Colours

Fill in the missing letters to complete the colour

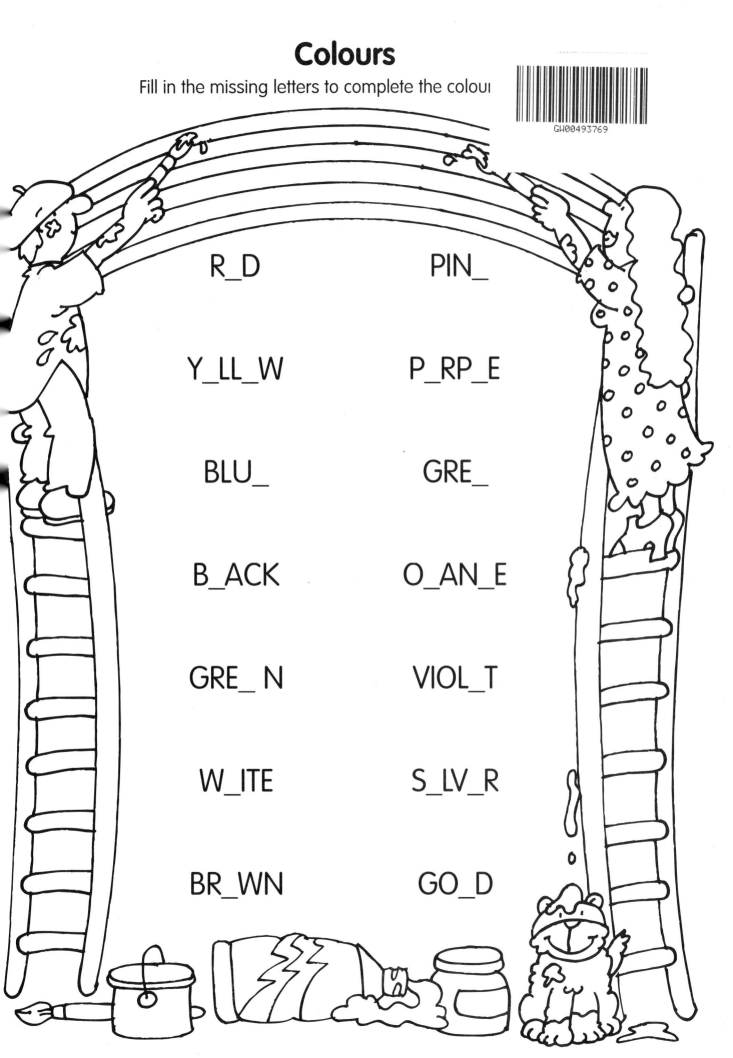

R_D

PIN_

Y_LL_W

P_RP_E

BLU_

GRE_

B_ACK

O_AN_E

GRE_ N

VIOL_T

W_ITE

S_LV_R

BR_WN

GO_D

First letters

Complete these spellings.

___own

___iends

___ain

___uit

___ost

___oe

___ue

___ildren

___umb

___irt

___eese

___air

___ower

___ocolate

Last letters

Complete these spellings.

carr___

mo___

pla___

plan___

la___

comput___

spo___

rob___

bo___

ali___

wat___

clo___

mo___

fla___

dre___

chick___

Double trouble

Add the missing pairs of letters to complete these words.
Choose between **ff**, **ss** and **ll**.

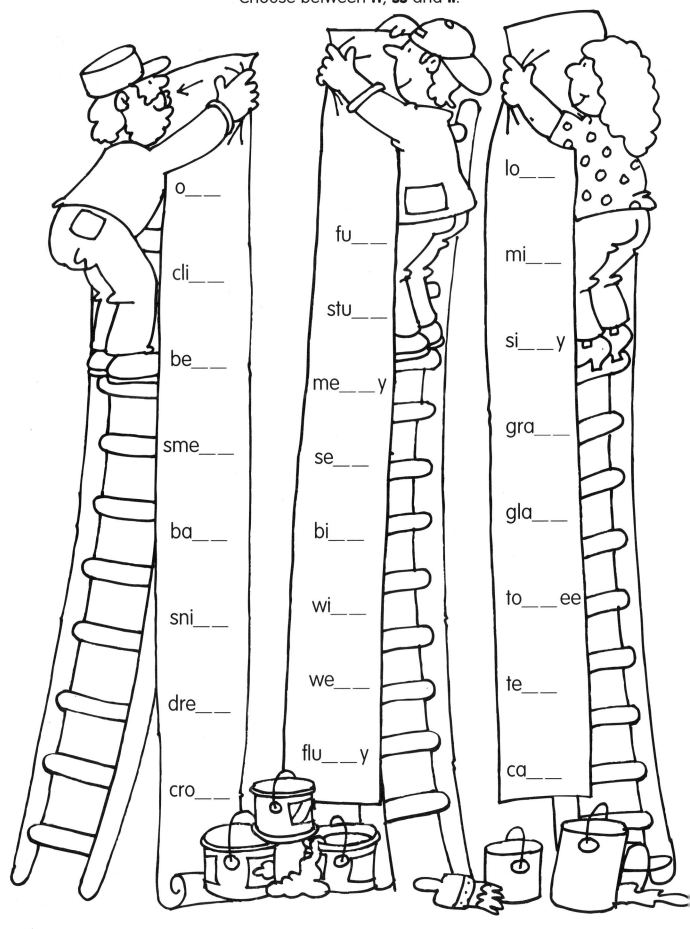

o___

cli___

be___

sme___

ba___

sni___

dre___

cro___

fu___

stu___

me___y

se___

bi___

wi___

we___

flu___y

lo___

mi___

si___y

gra___

gla___

to___ee

te___

ca___

Missing vowels

Using the sentences as clues, add the missing vowels to complete the words.

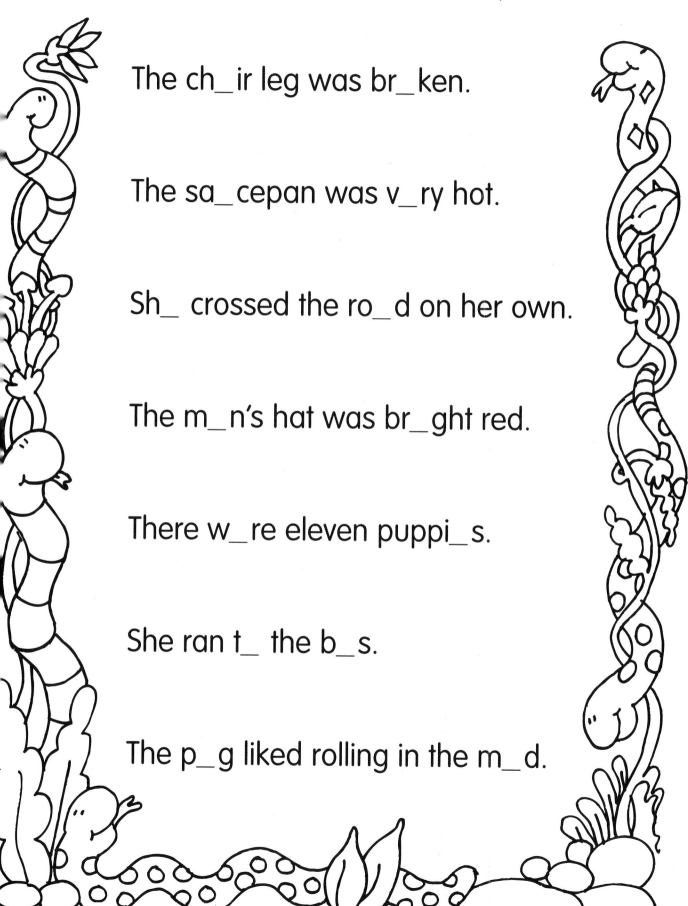

The ch_ir leg was br_ken.

The sa_cepan was v_ry hot.

Sh_ crossed the ro_d on her own.

The m_n's hat was br_ght red.

There w_re eleven puppi_s.

She ran t_ the b_s.

The p_g liked rolling in the m_d.

Rhyme time

Draw lines between the magicians' hats and the birds to join the pairs
of words that rhyme.

lift

free

blank

make

sheep

cake

keep

gift

tank

tree

Words with 'ow' or 'ou'

The letters **ow** and **ou** are different letters that can make the same sound.
Complete the words by writing the missing sound.

c _ _

s _ _ nd

_ _ t

t _ _ n

h _ _

l _ _ d

br _ _ n

n _ _

cr _ _ d

r _ _ nd

f _ _ nd

d _ _ n

Compound capers

A 'compound word' is a word made up of two or more smaller words.
For example, **bed + room = bedroom**. Draw lines to join the rockets with
the planets to make compound words.

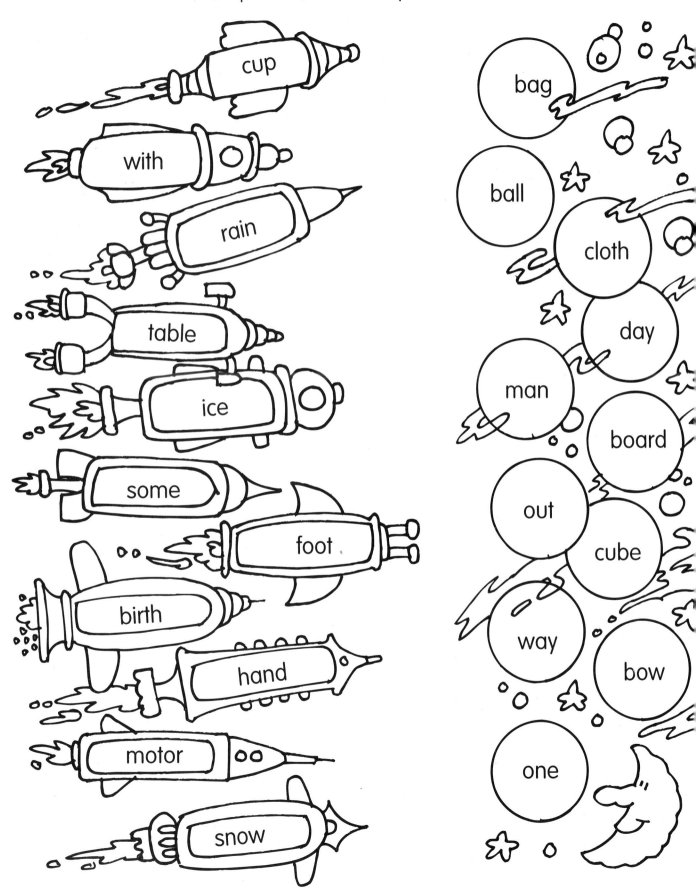

Wordsearch with 'wh'

Look for words beginning with **wh** in the wordsearch grid. You will find them by reading across or down. Draw a ring around the words as you find them.

```
W H I S K E R S H P
H A M L O P I W L K
O K W H E N B H A W
N W H I S T L E A K
W H A L E U O A L K
H I T E S C A T W H
E R F G H B H P H O
E J W H O L E N E H
L G A T E W S A R L
A D U G W H I T E S
```

Ssshhh... they're silent

All these words contain a silent letter **k**, **h** or **w**.
That means you write it but can't hear it when you say the word.
Fill in the missing silent letters to complete the words.

__rite

w__isper

__night

w__eel

__not

__our

w__istle

__rap

__nee

__nife

Tense time

Something that is happening now is written in the **present** tense: 'She climbs the ladder.'
Something that happened in the past is written in the **past** tense: 'She climbed the ladder.'
Complete the words in the **past** tense.

hear - hear__

laugh - laugh__ __

write - wr__te

run - r__n

come - c__me

drink - dr__nk

walk - walk__ __

jump - jump__ __

look - look__ __

clap - clapp__ __

smile - smile__

speak - sp__ke

hold - h__ld

see - s__ w

lift - lift__ __

rip - rip__ __d

carry - carr__ __d

hop - hopp__ __

talk - talk__ __

blink - blink__ __

Sounds the same

Some words sound the same but are spelt differently.
Add the missing letters to complete these pairs of same-sounding words.

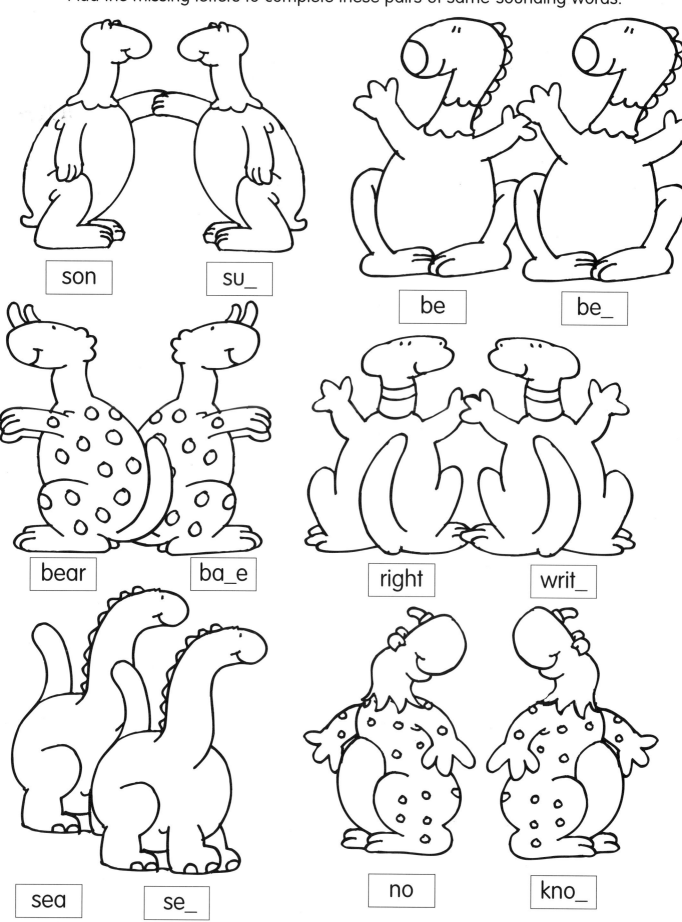

son   su_

be   be_

bear   ba_e

right   writ_

sea   se_

no   kno_

Making more

Change these words from **singular** to **plural** by adding the missing letters.

bird	→	bird_
witch	→	witch_ _
book	→	book_
mouse	→	m_ _e
foot	→	f_ _t
fox	→	fox_s
fairy	→	fair_ _ _
cloud	→	cloud _
house	→	house _
goose	→	g_ _se
thumb	→	thumb _

Double letter crossword

Using the pictures as clues, follow the numbers across and down, and write the words in the grid. All the words have the double letters **pp**, **rr** or **tt**.

Words with magic 'e'

Add or take away the letter **e** from these words to make new words.

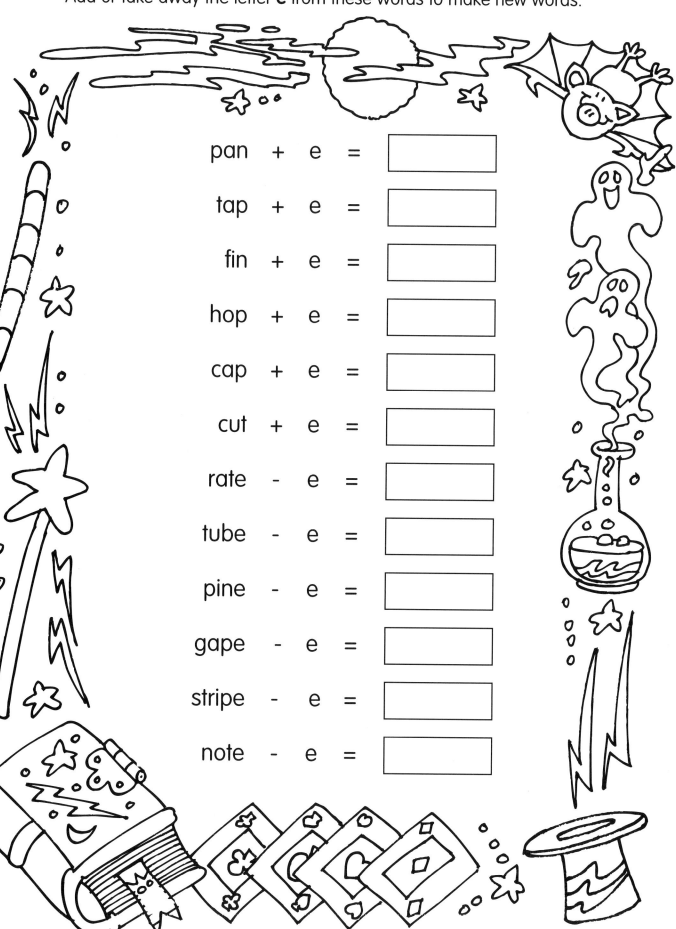

pan + e = ☐

tap + e = ☐

fin + e = ☐

hop + e = ☐

cap + e = ☐

cut + e = ☐

rate − e = ☐

tube − e = ☐

pine − e = ☐

gape − e = ☐

stripe − e = ☐

note − e = ☐

Answers

Colours
RED PINK YELLOW PURPLE BLUE GREY
BLACK ORANGE GREEN VIOLET WHITE
SILVER BROWN GOLD

First letters
crown friends train
fruit glue ghost
shoe children thumb
skirt chair cheese
flower chocolate

Last letters
carrot moth plant planet
lamp computer spoon
boat alien robot
watch clock moon
flask dress chicken

Double trouble
off	full/fuss	loss/loll
cliff	stuff	miss/mill
bell	messy	silly/sissy
smell	sell	grass
ball	bill	glass
sniff	will	toffee
dress	well	tell
cross	fluffy	call

Missing vowels
The chair leg was broken.
The saucepan was very hot.
She crossed the road on her own.
The man's hat was bright red.
There were eleven puppies.
She ran to the bus.
The pig liked rolling in the mud.

Rhyme time
lift - gift free - tree blank - tank make - cake
sheep - keep

Words with 'ow' or 'ou'
cow out sound town how loud now brown
crowd round found down

Compound capers
cupboard without rainbow tablecloth icecube
someone football birthday handbag
motorway snowman

Wordsearch with 'wh'

Ssshhh... they're silent
write whisper knight wheel knot hour whistle
wrap knee knife

Tense time
hear - heard smile - smiled laugh - laughed
speak - spoke write - wrote hold - held run - ran
see - saw come - came lift - lifted drink - drank
rip - ripped walk - walked carry - carried
jump - jumped hop - hopped look - looked
talk - talked clap - clapped blink - blinked

Sounds the same
son - sun be - bee bear - bare right - write
sea - see no - know

Making more
birds - birds	witch - witches
book - books	mouse - mice
foot - feet	fox - foxes
fairy - fairies	cloud - clouds
house - houses	goose - geese
thumb - thumbs	

Double letter crossword

Words with magic 'e'
pan + e = pane	tap + e = tape
fin + e = fine	hop + e = hope
cap + e = cape	cut + e = cute
rate - e = rat	tube - e = tub
pine - e = pin	gape - e = gap
stripe - e = strip	note - e = not